❄︎ **P**RESENTED ❄︎

TO

_____

BY

_____

ON

_____

. . . I have good news for you,
a message that will fill everyone with joy.
Today your Savior, Christ the Lord, was born . . .
Luke 2:10-11

Christmas
Moments
Readings for the
Christmas Season

Grand Rapids, Michigan 49418 U.S.A.

Developed and produced by The Livingstone Corporation. Project staff include: James C. Galvin, Jonathan Farrar, Christopher D. Hudson, Daryl J. Lucas, and Brenda Todd. Prayers written by Michael Kendrick.

Cover design by JMK Associates.

The illustrations found in this book are the work of German artists who created these woodcuts prior to 1900. Artists include: Julius Schnorr von Carolsfeld, G. Jäger, F. Overbeck, U. Rethel, J. von Vührich, and others.

ISBN 0-529-10470-9

Library of Congress Catalog Card Number 95-61688

Published by: World Publishing, Inc.
                    Grand Rapids, Michigan 49418 U.S.A.
                    All rights reserved.

Printed in the United States of America

1 2 3 4 5 6 7 8 99 98 97 96 95

INTRODUCTION

Lights. Decorations. Shopping. Gifts. Parties. Concerts. Christmas is a wonderful season. Unfortunately, all the pleasures and activities of the holiday season can prevent us from considering the real meaning behind this season.

The real meaning of Christmas centers on a real child who was born into a real world. Christmas celebrates the time that

God entered the human race and brought salvation to the world. Because of that first Christmas, we have the opportunity for eternal life.

Christmas, then, isn't about lights, holly, or ivy. It means more than parties, decorations, and gift-giving. The true meaning of Christmas was captured by an angel who brought good news to a handful of Jewish shepherds, "I have good news for you, a message that will fill everyone with joy. Today your Savior, Christ the Lord, was born."

Our prayer is that over the next twenty-five days, *Christmas Moments* will help you and your family focus on the real meaning of Christmas.

DECEMBER 1
The Word Becomes Human

¹In the beginning the Word already existed. The Word was with God, and the Word was God. ²He was already with God in the beginning.

³Everything came into existence through him. Not one thing that exists was made without him.

⁴He was the source of life, and that life was the light for humanity.

⁵ The light shines in the dark, and the dark has never extinguished it.

⁹ The real light, which shines on everyone, was coming into the world. ¹⁰He was in the world, and the world came into existence through him. Yet, the world didn't recognize him. ¹¹He went to his own people, and his own people didn't accept him. ¹²However, he gave the right to become God's children to everyone who believed in him. ¹³ These are people who haven't been born in a physical way—from a human impulse or from a husband's desire ₍to have a child₎. Their birth was from God.

¹⁴ The Word became human and lived among us. We saw his glory. It was the glory that the Father shares with his only Son, a glory full of kindness and truth.

John 1:1-5, 9-14

Lord, we honor you today for your eternal splendor.
You are the mighty creator,
the source of life,
the light that shines in the dark.
Yet you became human and lived among us
so that we might become your children.
Let your glory fill our lives,
the glory full of kindness and truth.

DECEMBER 2
Jesus Will Be Born in Bethlehem

² You, Bethlehem Ephrathah,
   are too small to be included among Judah's cities.
      Yet, from you Israel's future ruler will come for me.

His origins go back to the distant past,
to days long ago.
3 That is why the LORD will abandon Israel
until the time a mother has a child.
Then the rest of the LORD's people will return
to the people of Israel.
4 The child will become the shepherd of his flock.
ₗHe will lead themⱼ with the strength of the LORD,
with the majestic name of the LORD his God.
They will live in safety
because his greatness will reach the ends
of the earth.
5 This man will be their peace.

Micah 5:2-5

Merciful God, you chose a humble village in Judea
to display your authority and power.
Even now, your Son is bringing people to you.
Like a shepherd, you watch over us, keeping us safe
from harm. More than that,
you fill us with peace that is not found on earth.
May your greatness continue to reach
the ends of the earth.

DECEMBER 3
The Angel Gabriel Appears to Zechariah

⁵When Herod was king of Judea, there was a priest named Zechariah, who belonged to the division of priests named after Abijah. Zechariah's wife Elizabeth was a descendant of Aaron. ⁶Zechariah and Elizabeth had God's approval. They followed all the Lord's commands and regulations perfectly. ⁷ Yet, they never had any children because Elizabeth couldn't become pregnant. Both of them were too old to have children.

⁸Zechariah was on duty with his division of priests. As he served in God's presence, ⁹he was chosen by priestly custom to go into the Lord's temple to burn incense. ¹⁰All the people were praying outside while he was burning incense.

¹¹ Then, to the right of the incense altar, an angel of the Lord appeared to him. ¹²Zechariah was troubled and overcome with fear.

¹³ The angel said to him, "Don't be afraid, Zechariah! God has heard your prayer. Your wife Elizabeth will have a

son, and you will name him John. [14]He will be your pride and joy, and many people will be glad that he was born. [15]As far as the Lord is concerned, he will be a great man. He will never drink wine or any other liquor. He will be filled with the Holy Spirit even before he is born. [16]He will bring many people in Israel back to the Lord their God. [17]He will go ahead of the Lord with the spirit and power that Elijah had. He will change parents' attitudes toward their children. He will change disobedient people so that they will accept the wisdom of those who have God's approval. In this way he will prepare the people for their Lord."

Luke 1:5-17

Heavenly Father, you are always amazing us
with your goodness and compassion.
You hear our prayers and delight in answering
our requests, even though we are unworthy
and often lacking in faith.
Prepare our hearts as we celebrate the coming of your Son.

DECEMBER 4
Zechariah Doubts Gabriel's Message

[18]Zechariah said to the angel, "What proof is there for this? I'm an old man, and my wife is beyond her childbearing years."

[19] The angel answered him, "I'm Gabriel! I stand in God's presence. God sent me to tell you this good news. [20]But because you didn't believe what I said, you will be unable to talk until the day this happens. Everything will come true at the right time."

[21]Meanwhile, the people were waiting for Zechariah. They were amazed that he was staying in the temple so long. [22]When he did come out, he was unable to speak to them. So they realized that he had seen a vision in the temple. He motioned to them but remained unable to talk.

[23]When the days of his service were over, he went home. [24]Later, his wife Elizabeth became pregnant and didn't go

out in public for five months. She said, [25]"The Lord has done this for me now. He has removed my public disgrace."

Luke 1:18-25

Lord God, thank you for working
mighty deeds that defy impossible odds
and bring honor to your name.
Help us to always believe your life-giving message.
May our speech reflect confidence in your promises.
Thank you also for removing our disgrace
and restoring us to fellowship with you.

DECEMBER 5
The Angel Gabriel Comes to Mary

[26]Six months after Elizabeth had become pregnant, God sent the angel Gabriel to Nazareth, a city in Galilee. [27] The angel went to a virgin promised in marriage to a

descendant of David named Joseph. The virgin's name was Mary.

[28]When the angel entered her home, he greeted her and said, "You are favored by the Lord! The Lord is with you."

[29]She was startled by what the angel said and tried to figure out what this greeting meant.

[30] The angel told her,

> "Don't be afraid, Mary. You have found favor
> with God.
> [31] You will become pregnant, give birth to a son,
> and name him Jesus.
> [32] He will be a great man
> and will be called the Son of the Most High.
>
> The Lord God will give him
> the throne of his ancestor David.
> [33] Your son will be king of Jacob's people forever,
> and his kingdom will never end."

Luke 1:26-33

Dear Father, the news you announce
fills us with wonder and hope.
Your Son was born of a virgin in lowly surroundings.
He came because of his boundless love for us,
and that love cost him his life.
You have raised him up,
and now he is honored above all names.
His kingdom will never end.
Let us constantly praise you.

❄　　❄　　❄

DECEMBER 6
Jesus' Mother Will Be a Virgin

³⁴Mary asked the angel, "How can this be? I've never had sexual intercourse."

³⁵ The angel answered her, "The Holy Spirit will come to you, and the power of the Most High will overshadow you. Therefore, the holy child developing inside you will be called the Son of God.

³⁶"Elizabeth, your relative, is six months pregnant with a son in her old age. People said she couldn't have a child. ³⁷But nothing is impossible for God."

³⁸Mary answered, "I am the Lord's servant. Let everything you've said happen to me."

Then the angel left her.

Luke 1:34-38

Our defender and Savior, nothing
is impossible for you.
You spoke the world into existence,
you delivered your people with great miracles, and you
saved us from sin through the sacrifice of your Son.
May we follow the example of your servant Mary
by humbly trusting you.

❄   ❄   ❄

DECEMBER 7
An Angel Appears to Joseph

¹⁸The birth of Jesus Christ took place in this way. His mother Mary had been promised to Joseph in marriage.

But before they were married, Mary realized that she was pregnant by the Holy Spirit. [19]Her husband Joseph was an honorable man and did not want to disgrace her publicly. So he decided to break the marriage agreement with her secretly.

[20]Joseph had this in mind when an angel of the Lord appeared to him in a dream. The angel said to him, "Joseph, descendant of David, don't be afraid to take Mary as your wife. She is pregnant by the Holy Spirit. [21]She will give birth to a son, and you will name him Jesus [He Saves], because he will save his people from their sins." [22]All this happened so that what the Lord had spoken through the prophet came true: [23]"The virgin will become pregnant and give birth to a son, and they will name him Immanuel," which means "God is with us."

[24]When Joseph woke up, he did what the angel of the Lord had commanded him to do. He took Mary to be his wife. [25]He did not have marital relations with her before she gave birth to a son.

Matthew 1:18-25

Father, you have come to us and now live with us.
You have encouraged us with your counsel.
You are faithful to your promises.
You are forgiving to your people.
Help us determine to do what you have commanded.

❄   ❄   ❄

DECEMBER 8
Mary Visits Elizabeth

[39]Soon afterward, Mary hurried to a city in the mountain region of Judah. [40]She entered Zechariah's home and greeted Elizabeth.

[41]When Elizabeth heard the greeting, she felt the baby kick. Elizabeth was filled with the Holy Spirit. [42]She said in a loud voice, "You are the most blessed of all women, and blessed is the child that you will have. [43]I feel blessed that the mother of my Lord is visiting me. [44]As

soon as I heard your greeting, I felt the baby jump for joy. ⁴⁵You are blessed for believing that the Lord would keep his promise to you."

Luke 1:39-45

God of joy and fulfillment,
we are indeed blessed when we trust in your promises.
Let the celebration of your arrival
cause us to sing praise to you,
Father, Son, and Holy Spirit.
Blessing, honor, and glory are yours now and forever.

DECEMBER 9
Mary Praises God

⁴⁶Mary said,

"My soul praises the Lord's greatness!
⁴⁷ My spirit finds its joy in God, my Savior,
⁴⁸ because he has looked favorably on me,
his humble servant.

"From now on, all people will call me blessed
49   because the Almighty has done great things to me.
        His name is holy.
50   For those who fear him,
                his mercy lasts throughout every generation.

51   "He displayed his mighty power.
        He scattered those who think too highly
            of themselves.
52   He pulled strong rulers from their thrones.
            He honored humble people.
53   He fed hungry people with good food.
                He sent rich people away with nothing.

54   "He remembered to help his servant Israel forever.
55   This is the promise he made to our ancestors,
            to Abraham and his descendants."

56Mary stayed with Elizabeth about three months and
then went back home.

Luke 1:46-56

Lord, you are worthy of every tribute
on earth and in heaven.
You control the destinies of kings and rulers.

You show compassion to the poor and the hungry.
Nothing happens that your watchful eye does not see.
Above all, you have delivered us from our sin.
Let us find our joy in you today.

❄   ❄   ❄

DECEMBER 10
John Is Born

[57] When the time came for Elizabeth to have her child, she gave birth to a son. [58]Her neighbors and relatives heard that the Lord had been very kind to her, and they shared her joy.

[59]When the child was eight days old, they went ⌊to the temple⌋ to circumcise him. They were going to name him Zechariah after his father. [60]But his mother spoke up, "Absolutely not! His name will be John."

[61]Their friends said to her, "But you don't have any relatives with that name."

[62]So they motioned to the baby's father to see what he

wanted to name the child. ⁶³Zechariah asked for a writing tablet and wrote, "His name is John." Everyone was amazed.

⁶⁴Suddenly, Zechariah was able to speak, and he began to praise God.

⁶⁵All their neighbors were filled with awe. Throughout the mountain region of Judea, people talked about everything that had happened. ⁶⁶Everyone who heard about it seriously thought it over and asked, "What does the future hold for this child?" It was clear that the Lord was with him.

Luke 1:57-66

Heavenly Father, the world is astonished by your gift
of salvation. Teach us to obey
and remain faithful so that others will
acknowledge your greatness and share in our joy.
Let others see your Spirit at work within us
so that they may long to know you.

DECEMBER 11
Zechariah's Prophecy About Jesus

[67]His father Zechariah was filled with the Holy Spirit and prophesied,

[68] "Praise the Lord God of Israel!
    He has come to take care of his people
      and to set them free.
[69] He has raised up a mighty Savior for us
    in the family of his servant David.
[70] He made this promise through his holy prophets
      long ago.
[71] He promised to save us from our enemies
    and from the power of all who hate us.
[72] He has shown his mercy to our ancestors
    and remembered his holy promise,
[73]   the oath that he swore to our ancestor Abraham.
[74] He promised to rescue us from our enemies' power
    so that we could serve him without fear
[75]   by being holy and honorable as long as we live."

Luke 1:67-75

Eternal God, you have given us a mighty Savior
to care for us and to set us free.
What was promised to the prophets was fulfilled in the life,
death, and resurrection of your holy Son.
We can be spared from our enemies
and serve you without fear.
Let us praise you by following the words
of Zechariah and by living holy lives.

❄   ❄   ❄

DECEMBER 12

Zechariah's Prophecy About John

76 "You, child, will be called a prophet of the Most High.
You will go ahead of the Lord to prepare his way.
77 You will make his people know that they can be saved
through the forgiveness of their sins.
78 A new day will dawn on us from above
because our God is loving and merciful.

79   He will give light to those who live in the dark
      and in death's shadow.
   He will guide us into the way of peace."

80 The child John grew and became spiritually strong. He lived in the desert until the day he appeared to the people of Israel.

Luke 1:76-80

Dear Lord, the new day of salvation is here,
and we lift our voices in praise.
The darkness of sin has been overcome,
and a radiant light floods the world.
Keep our hearts and minds alert
as we remember the arrival of your Son.
May we desire to show to others
the love and mercy you have shown to us.

DECEMBER 13
Jesus Is Born

¹At that time the Emperor Augustus ordered a census of the Roman Empire. ² This was the first census taken while Quirinius was governor of Syria. ³All the people went to register in the cities where their ancestors had lived.

⁴So Joseph went from Nazareth, a city in Galilee, to a Judean city called Bethlehem. Joseph, a descendant of King David, went to Bethlehem because David had been born there. ⁵Joseph went there to register with Mary. She had been promised to him in marriage and was pregnant.

⁶ While they were in Bethlehem, the time came for Mary to have her child. ⁷She gave birth to her firstborn son. She wrapped him in strips of cloth and laid him in a manger because there wasn't any room for them in the inn.

Luke 2:1-7

Mighty God, amid the busyness of the world's affairs,
you are at work providing salvation for all people.
What the world sees as insignificant and trivial
you have invested with great meaning.
You brought your Son into the world
in humble circumstances.
He lived among us and died an agonizing death
so that we might inherit your kingdom.
May we give you the glory and majesty you deserve, O Lord.

❄   ❄   ❄

DECEMBER 14

Angels Announce the Birth of Jesus

[8]Shepherds were in the fields near Bethlehem. They were taking turns watching their flock during the night. [9]An angel from the Lord suddenly appeared to them. The glory of the Lord filled the area with light, and they were terrified. [10] The angel said to them, "Don't be afraid! I have good news for you, a message that will fill

everyone with joy. [11]Today your Savior, Christ the Lord, was born in David's city. [12] This is how you will recognize him: You will find an infant wrapped in strips of cloth and lying in a manger."

[13]Suddenly, a large army of angels appeared with the angel. They were praising God by saying,

[14]   "Glory to God in the highest heaven,
          and on earth peace to those who have his good will!"

Luke 2:8-14

Father, we long for the glory of your presence.
The news of our Savior's birth fills us with joy.
Our words of praise join with the voices of the angels who
proclaim your greatness day and night.
Grant us your peace as we eagerly await the day
when we will be with you
in a new heaven and new earth

DECEMBER 15
Shepherds Visit Baby Jesus

¹⁵ The angels left them and went back to heaven. The shepherds said to each other, "Let's go to Bethlehem and see what the Lord has told us about."

¹⁶ They went quickly and found Mary and Joseph with the baby, who was lying in a manger. ¹⁷ When they saw the child, they repeated what they had been told about him. ¹⁸Everyone who heard the shepherds' story was amazed.

¹⁹Mary treasured all these things in her heart and always thought about them.

²⁰As the shepherds returned to their flock, they glorified and praised God for everything they had seen and heard. Everything happened the way the angel had told them.

Luke 2:15-20

God of all comfort, you invite us
to follow your direction so that we may see your goodness.
Encourage us with with the knowledge that Jesus' birth in

that Bethlehem stable reclaims our lives from sin.
We will treasure the memory
of your wondrous acts and think about them often.

❄   ❄   ❄

DECEMBER 16
Jesus' Parents Obey Moses' Teachings

²¹Eight days after his birth, the child was circumcised and named Jesus. This was the name the angel had given him before his mother became pregnant.

²²After the days required by Moses' Teachings to make a mother clean had passed, Joseph and Mary went to Jerusalem. They took Jesus to present him to the Lord. ²³ They did exactly what was written in the Lord's Teachings: "Every firstborn boy is to be set apart as holy to the Lord." ²⁴They also offered a sacrifice as required by the Lord's Teachings: "a pair of mourning doves or two young pigeons."

Luke 2:21-24

Our God and Savior, your Son was named "Jesus."
In this way we remember that he came
to save us from our sin.
He was holy, set apart, without blemish.
Yet he willingly became a perfect sacrifice.
We praise you for surrounding us
with such mercy and forgiveness.

❄   ❄   ❄

DECEMBER 17
Simeon's Prophecy

[25]A man named Simeon was in Jerusalem. He lived an honorable and devout life. He was waiting for the one who would comfort Israel. The Holy Spirit was with Simeon [26]and had told him that he wouldn't die until he had seen the Messiah, whom the Lord would send.

[27]Moved by the Spirit, Simeon went into the temple courtyard. Mary and Joseph were bringing the child Jesus into the courtyard at the same time. They brought

him so that they could do for him what Moses'
Teachings required. ²⁸Then Simeon took the child in his
arms and praised God by saying,

²⁹ "Now, Lord, you are allowing your servant
      to leave in peace
    as you promised.
³⁰ My eyes have seen your salvation,
³¹   which you have prepared for all people to see.

³²   He is a light that will reveal ⌊salvation⌋
         to the nations
       and bring glory to your people Israel."

³³Jesus' father and mother were amazed at what was said
about him. ³⁴Then Simeon blessed them and said to
Mary, his mother, "This child is the reason that many
people in Israel will be condemned and many others will
be saved. He will be a sign that will expose ³⁵the
thoughts of those who reject him. And a sword will
pierce your heart."

Luke 2:25-35

We thank you, Lord,
that you refresh us when we are weary.
You are the light to all nations and the glory of Israel.
You involve those who love you in your plan of salvation
and allow them to see the fulfillment of your promises.
You comfort those who seek your goodness.
Keep our hearts filled with the hope
that Simeon carried so long ago.

DECEMBER 18
Anna's Prophecy

[36]Anna, a prophet, was also there. She was a descendant of Phanuel from the tribe of Asher. She was now very old. Her husband had died seven years after they were married, [37]and she had been a widow for 84 years. Anna never left the temple courtyard but worshiped day and night by fasting and praying. [38]At that moment she came

up to Mary and Joseph and began to thank God. She spoke about Jesus to all who were waiting for Jerusalem to be set free.

[39]After doing everything the Lord's Teachings required, Joseph and Mary returned to their hometown of Nazareth in Galilee. [40] The child grew and became strong. He was filled with wisdom, and God's favor was with him.

Luke 2:36-40

O God, our king and lord, we praise your holy name.
As Anna honored you by worshiping in the temple
day and night, let us also please you with lives
that conform to your will.
Help us proclaim to others the good news
that Jesus came to set us free from our sins.
Give us thankful hearts also so that we will not
take your provision for granted.

DECEMBER 19
The Wise Men Visit

¹Jesus was born in Bethlehem in Judea when Herod was king. After Jesus' birth wise men from the east arrived in Jerusalem. ²They asked, "Where is the one who was born to be the king of the Jews? We saw his star rising and have come to worship him."

³When King Herod and all Jerusalem heard about this, they became disturbed. ⁴He called together all the chief priests and scribes and tried to find out from them where the Messiah was supposed to be born.

⁵ They told him, "In Bethlehem in Judea. The prophet wrote about this:

⁶   Bethlehem in the land of Judah,
        you are by no means least among the leaders
           of Judah.
        A leader will come from you.
        He will shepherd my people Israel."

Matthew 2:1-6

Heavenly Father, it is good to seek you and worship you.
You have drawn people from every land
who have left everything to follow you and adore you.
Cleanse us from sin so that we too might
worship you without hindrance.
Guide us daily .

DECEMBER 20
The Wise Men Bring Gifts

[7] Then Herod secretly called the wise men and found out from them exactly when the star had appeared. [8] As he sent them to Bethlehem, he said, "Go and search carefully for the child. When you have found him, report to me so that I may go and worship him too."

[9] After they had heard the king, they started out. The star they had seen rising led them until it stopped over the place where the child was. [10] They were overwhelmed with joy to see the star. [11] When they

entered the house, they saw the child with his mother Mary. So they bowed down and worshiped him. Then they opened their treasure chests and offered him gifts of gold, frankincense, and myrrh.

¹²God warned them in a dream not to go back to Herod. So they left for their country by another road.

Matthew 2:7-12

Almighty God, your people are
overwhelmed with joy at your appearance.
Let us not pretend to give you honor as Herod did.
Instead, let us offer gifts that are precious to you,
lives of obedience and purity.

❄   ❄   ❄

DECEMBER 21
The Escape to Egypt

¹³After they had left, an angel of the Lord appeared to Joseph in a dream. The angel said to him, "Get up, take the child and his mother, and flee to Egypt. Stay there

until I tell you, because Herod intends to search for the child and kill him."

¹⁴Joseph got up, took the child and his mother, and left for Egypt that night. ¹⁵He stayed there until Herod died. What the Lord had spoken through the prophet came true: "I have called my son out of Egypt."

Matthew 2:13-15

God of mercy, we thank you for
protecting us day and night.
You guard your children with infinite care.
You keep us safe from those who try to harm us.
You deliver us from our enemies.
May we place our complete trust in you,
for you are our only refuge.

DECEMBER 22
Herod Tries to Kill Jesus

[16]When Herod saw that the wise men had tricked him, he became furious. He sent soldiers to kill all the boys two years old and younger in or near Bethlehem. This matched the exact time he had learned from the wise men. [17] Then the words spoken through the prophet Jeremiah came true:

[18] "A sound was heard in Ramah,
    the sound of crying in bitter grief.
        Rachel was crying for her children.
        She refused to be comforted
            because they were dead."

Matthew 2:16-18

Lord, you came into the world to
overthrow the powers of darkness.
Even though we see suffering and evil,
we acknowledge that one day you will wipe away our tears

and bring about a new world.
Victory is yours, O Lord.
May all creation praise your might and justice.

❄   ❄   ❄

DECEMBER 23
From Egypt to Nazareth

¹⁹After Herod was dead, an angel of the Lord appeared in a dream to Joseph in Egypt. ²⁰ The angel said to him, "Get up, take the child and his mother, and go to Israel. Those who tried to kill the child are dead."

²¹Joseph got up, took the child and his mother, and went to Israel. ²²But when he heard that Archelaus had succeeded his father Herod as king of Judea, Joseph was afraid to go there. Warned in a dream, he left for Galilee ²³and made his home in a city called Nazareth. So what the prophets had said came true: "He will be called a Nazarene."

Matthew 2:19-23

Heavenly Father, you are a faithful guide.
You warn us of danger and keep us from falling.
During Christmas, as we continue our spiritual journey,
help us to trust more completely
in your great wisdom and boundless love.

❄   ❄   ❄

DECEMBER 24

A Child Will Be Born as the Prince of Peace

² The people who walk in darkness will see a bright light.
The light will shine on those who live in the land
of death's shadow.

³ You will expand the nation and increase its happiness.
It will be happy in your presence
like those who celebrate the harvest
or rejoice when dividing loot.

⁴ You will break the yoke that burdens them,
the bar that is across their shoulders,
and the stick used by their oppressor,
as ⌊you did in the battle against⌋ Midian.

⁵ Every warrior's boot marching to the sound of battle
   and every garment rolled in blood
      will be burned as fuel in the fire.
⁶ A child will be born for us.
  A son will be given to us.
     The government will rest on his shoulders.
     He will be named:
        Wonderful Counselor,
        Mighty God,
        Everlasting Father,
        Prince of Peace.

Isaiah 9:2-6

Lord, we are happy in your presence.
You bless us and make us whole.
You are a Wonderful Counselor,
bestowing wisdom on those who love you;
the Mighty God, whose power is unmatched;
the Everlasting Father,
caring for his children from generation to generation;
and the Prince of Peace,
ending all strife and reconciling us to God.
Let us meditate today on your greatness.

December 25
God Has Spoken to Us Through His Son

[1]In the past God spoke to our ancestors at many different times and in many different ways through the prophets. [2]In these last days he has spoken to us through his Son. God made his Son responsible for everything. His Son is the one through whom God made the universe. [3]His Son is the reflection of God's glory and the exact likeness of God's being. He holds everything together through his powerful words. After he had cleansed people from their sins, he received the highest position, the one next to the Father in heaven.

[4] The Son has become greater than the angels since he has been given a name that is superior to theirs. [5]God never said to any of his angels,

"You are my Son.
Today I have become your Father."

And God never said to any of his angels,

"I will be his Father,
and he will be my Son."

[6]When God was about to send his firstborn Son into the world, he said,

"All of God's angels must worship him."

Hebrews 1:1-6

Eternal God, today we honor your Son.
We praise you, the Word made human,
for redeeming us and your creation.
Your majesty is proclaimed in heaven and on earth.
Everything belongs to you and is subject to you;
the angels kneel in adoration before you.
Let our praise resound everywhere.
The child of Bethlehem reigns as the King of Kings!

If you have enjoyed *Christmas Moments*, you may wish to consider using another Bible or devotional book that uses the *GOD'S WORD*™ text for the Bible. *GOD'S WORD*™ is the best-selling Bible translation that delivers God's message in crystal clear English.

Other *GOD'S WORD*™ products published by God's Word to the Nations Bible Society and World Publishing are available at your local Christian bookstore.